Musings of a Pilgrim

Musings on Advent

For Rachael

Contents

FOREWARD

I am glad I came upon James' musings although I cannot recall the first time that I came upon them. I know a musing appeared as a Facebook post and I was drawn to read it. Here were someone's reflections that were disarmingly undemanding. By that I mean they were unusually not 'agenda loaded'. There was no hidden persuasion to join the author to think like him or to agree, to feel sad for him or to share his emotions. Yet I knew that I was invited to reflect with him. I soon found myself looking forward to the next musing.

The title James had chosen is most apt. They are indeed 'musings' and we find ourselves walking with him – a pilgrim. I could imagine myself on a pilgrim's walk, coming upon this other pilgrim, falling into step with him and listening to his soliloquy or ruminative dialogue.

Almost Psalm-like, some musings bring the reader through moments of elation and our spirits are lifted while others cry out for answers on a range of issues: suffering, injustice, abuse of power and position, hurt, and grief. They are Psalm-like also because this pilgrim bears his soul as a spiritual being, who speaks of God and to God. He praises God and remonstrates with God. He allows his spirit to acknowledge God's blessings although there are as many times when darkness and silence are his companions.

From time to time, James brings us into the depth of his musings. Like this one as he finds his assumptions are dispelled while walking bare feet across the sands to Lindisfarne Island. He sees with the eyes of the Prophet Ezekiel: "*Then he brought me back to the entrance of the temple; there, water was flowing from below the threshold of the temple towards the east (for the temple faced east); and the water was flowing down from below the south end of the threshold of the temple, south of the altar.*" James found himself journeying with Ezekiel, describing a vision he had of a river flowing from the very throne of God, getting deeper and deeper until it was deep enough to swim in.

Thank you, James.

I commend *The Musings of A Pilgrim* to you.

The Reverend Canon Eileen Harrop
Diocese of Durham

ACKNOWLEDGEMENTS

There are so many people that deserve to be mentioned and thanked it would be impossible to name them all. Some of them I couldn't. They and I have passed momentarily, perhaps only with one overheard comment. So instead I will be very brief and mention only 4.

I would like to thank Eileen Harrop whose prodding set me off on a journey in early 2018 that I am still on, who has encouraged me on the way and who encouraged me to write this book. Also for writing the foreward. I will be forever grateful.

Various people prodded me in those early days: Catherine and Mike Simpson, and Charlie Scott-King, thank you for your encouragement.

Anthony Coulls: I always appreciate our chats and I know that, whilst you say things in a light manner, they are full of wisdom. Thank you for being there and for being a good friend.

Hannah and Rebekah, the best 2 daughters I could hope to have. You inspire me and make me want to be a better person and to make this a better place for you. And no list of thanks would be complete without mentioning Rachael, the most wonderful, beautiful person I know. I call it a privilege to be your husband. Thank you for all your encouragement and support, even when some of the things I do seem slightly crazy. Without the knowledge that you are there loving me, this whole journey would be so much more difficult. So, thank you from the bottom of my heart.

INTRODUCTION

Two and a half years ago I was asked what Pilgrimage meant to me. I started by writing:

Traditionally a pilgrimage was a journey to a holy place. Often a place claiming to have something special, a splinter of the True Cross, the chains that held Peter while he was in prison (they can be seen at San Pietro in Vincoli in Rome). Or somewhere where some special event had happened, like the appearance of a vision of Mary the mother of Jesus at Lourdes. It was believed that if you prayed at these shrines, you might be forgiven for your sins and have more chance of going to heaven.

Pilgrimages still happen today. People travel to the Shrine of Our Lady at Walsingham, or to Santiago de Compostela or St Cuthbert's Way to Lindisfarne.

These pilgrimages are often more than just the end point. The journey is also important. It may involve some form of penance. It could be because of the people you meet and interact with, whether they encourage, challenge or are purely good company. It could be as simple as enjoying walking and the view. Getting away from everyday life. There are many reasons, methods and end results.

But a pilgrimage does not have to be a physical journey. It does not have to start in physical place A and end up in physical place B. For me the real reason for a pilgrimage is the change it brings about in a person. It is someone starting off as person A and then changing, while somehow remaining the same person. The rough edges get knocked off. They grow, mature, develop new skills and enhance older ones. Priorities change so that what was once important now gets dropped, while something else which was not considered before becomes all consuming.

I started writing Musings of a Pilgrim back in 2015. In some ways it was more me trying to get my thoughts in order as I found writing things down very helpful. There was never any great plan to do anything with them. I guess I was expecting to write half a dozen and then stop. But things don't always work out how you expect them to.

I realised I was on a journey. I didn't – and still don't – know where I am heading. But that is not important. What is important is what happens on the way. The questions I ask. The path I take. The way that I change and develop. And Musings of a Pilgrim charts that journey. I use it often to clarify my thoughts, or to realise that I don't really know. That I have more questions than answers. And to realise that is OK. Sometimes all we can do is focus on the next step, rather than the whole staircase. Sometimes it is just as well the staircase turns out of sight, so we don't know what is coming. And that is OK.

Here is a snapshot of the Musings. I wrote these for Advent 2020. Rethink Church produced a word for each day. The idea was to post a photo based on the word for the day, but I wrote a reflection instead. I know that as I have re-read them I have been both encouraged and challenged. I pray that you also will find them beneficial in some way.

Don't let the entire staircase overwhelm you. Just focus on the next step.

TENDER

Tenderness is often associated with mothers. It feels appropriate to start these thoughts with Mary, the mother of Jesus. She was the one who "treasured up all these things [that the shepherds said] and pondered them in her heart." She was the one who, after having searched for 3 days to discover that her 12-year-old son was debating with the teachers in the temple, asked, "Son, why have you treated us like this? Your father and I have been anxiously searching for you." I cannot read that with any anger in her voice. Just relief and love. And she was one who was broken when she watched him die on the cross.

But one phrase sticks out for me. She has just been told that, as an unmarried mid-teenage woman, she would become pregnant and give birth. Even if these days that is not too uncommon, 2000 years ago in Palestine it was a big no-no. She could have become an outcast. It was likely that her family and friends would have wanted nothing more to do with her. She would have had virtually no chance of finding a husband worth the name. She would have had very few prospects in life.

Yet what was her reaction? "I am the Lord's servant. May your word to me be fulfilled."

She faced ridicule and being ostracised. "I am the Lord's servant. May your word to me be fulfilled."

Her life was, potentially, over before it had really begun. "I am the Lord's servant. May your word to me be fulfilled."

Those are twelve of the most incredible words ever spoken. Mary, who faced ruin for something that she had no control over, was prepared to trust God and put her whole future in his hands. For Mary, the most important thing was her relationship with her God. It far outweighed everything else. She had a simple faith, and belief in what he said. The angel had said, "Do not be afraid." The angel had said that this was God's plan. And that was enough for Mary. She trusted what she was told, even if everything about it seemed impossible and wrong. "I am the Lord's servant. May your word to me be fulfilled."

It is one of the most incredible and powerful sentiments. We may find ourselves in difficult situations. We may find ourselves being asked to do something we dread. Something that seems impossible. Something where we can see only disaster. But if God asks us to do it, then we can be sure that it is the correct thing to do. We can be sure that God will be with us and that, somehow, he will work things out.

Let us say, with Mary, "I am the Lord's servant. May your word to me be fulfilled."

DELIVER

An angel appeared to Zechariah, to prophesy John's birth. The same angel, Gabriel, appeared to Mary to tell her she would become pregnant and give birth to the Son of God. God appeared to Joseph in a dream to reassure him that everything would be OK.

God delivered his messages to people in a variety of ways. With Moses it was a burning bush that did not burn up. With Joseph it was through dreams. With Elijah it was a still small voice. In the New Testament we have voices from heaven and visions.

And God has not stopped. He has so many ways of delivering his messages to his people. We can all wait for the big, impressive, impossible to miss sign. I would love to have an angel appear to me and pass on a word from God. I would love to see a hand writing a message on a wall. It can work that way, but not often. Often it is the still, small voice. The voice that we can so easily miss. The voice that we can dismiss as just my thoughts, if we take even that much notice of it. But God is still talking today. We just need to quieten our minds and spirits and focus on him. We need to come and sit at his feet and wait. We need to put aside time. We cannot keep rushing about, filling our lives with more and more activity, and expect to hear God's still, small voice. We need to put aside time to wait on him, to listen to what he is desperately trying to get through to us. It is so hard to do, but we must do it. We need to focus on our relationship with him above all else. We need to prioritise time with him. We need to open ourselves up to what he is saying. We need to be ready for it, whatever it is. And as we start doing that, we will hear that still, small voice. We will hear the message that he is delivering to us.

STRENGTHEN

Was it easy for Mary those long months before she gave birth? Was it easy with all the looks and gossip? She knew the truth. Joseph knew the truth. But was it easy? Did she ever waver in her belief? Did she ever doubt? Did she ever feel she did not have the strength to keep on?

I know I often waver. Everything is fine, then I suddenly realise how much I need to do, and I start panicking. I am facing an unpleasant situation, and it is all I can think about. The thoughts grow and grow until they are all-consuming, and I feel myself being crushed by them. I feel weak and helpless in the face of a giant.

Hebrews 12:1-2 states:

And let us run with perseverance the race marked out before us, fixing our eyes on Jesus, the pioneer and perfecter of faith.

I need to fix my eyes on Jesus. All too often my eyes are fixed on the problems. But when I manage to drag my eyes off the issues and focus on Jesus, I find a renewed strength. Sometimes the stress and worry can drain away. Sometimes the weight is lifted from my shoulders. Sometimes there is just the feeling that yes, this will be tough, but God is there with me, and he will see me through. We need to come and sit at the feet of Jesus and listen in wonder and amazement. We need to come to him and acknowledge our weakness and look for his strength. Because his strength has never and will never fail.

One of my favourite passages in Isaiah 40:30-31, where we read:

Even youths grow tired and weary,
and young men stumble and fall;
but those who hope in the Lord will renew their strength.
They will soar on wings like eagles;
they will run and not grow weary,
they will walk and not be faint.

Those who wait on the Lord. Not those who rush in, say a quick prayer and rush back out again. But those who wait. Those who linger. Those who spend time with him, listening, receiving from him. And the wider context of this passage? The creator God. The God who created the heavens and the earth is the same God who gives us strength to carry on when we wait on him. The same God who rules the universe is interested in me and wants to give me what I need, if only I will come to him in humility and receive.

So, did Mary struggle at all over those long months? I don't know. But I am sure she followed the Psalmist's advice and could make the same cry:

I lift my eyes to the mountains –
where does my help come from?
My help comes from the Lord,
the maker of heaven and earth.

EARTH

It may or may not have been a dirty, smelly stable that Jesus was born into. But it certainly was not a rich palace. His parents then went on the run for a period to protect him, for King Herod wanted to murder all the boys born in Bethlehem at the same time to ensure that the new King did not survive. It was not an easy introduction to life on planet Earth. It was a similar introduction to that had by many babies born in times of conflict or famine. An introduction filled with danger and uncertainty on many fronts. Certainly not an introduction of stability.

But think for a minute who this baby was and where he had come from. He was almighty God, being born as a baby boy. He had come from the riches of heaven, for which the bible uses the most amazing vocabulary to describe its riches and majesty, into a poor family which then went on the run. It was quite a change. God himself, living on earth among humankind. And then having to work for a living. Having to become a carpenter and get his hands dirty so that he could afford to eat, drink, and put a roof over his head. The creator, having to create again to survive.

It does not make any sense if we cut the story short. It is a cute tale, full of fluffy animals, but that is all. Why on earth would God come down to live with us? Why would he make it so that he had to have a trade on earth to survive? Why would he make it so that he had to suffer?

The answer is seen at the end of the story, with 3 wooden crosses. Jesus, God himself, left heaven and came to live on earth for one reason only. He came to die, and then rise to live again. It is not as cute and cuddly as the Christmas story, but that was the reason.

We were created to have a relationship with God. That is his desire for us all. He wants us to know him and to acknowledge him as God. But we have messed up and gone our own way. We have decided that we know better and that we do not need him. And that has caused God unimaginable pain. Think of that: my actions can cause the almighty God, the creator of the universe, unimaginable pain. My actions have destroyed that close, intimate relationship that he desires for us. Because God is just, that rebellion, that sin, needs punishment. But because God is loving and merciful, he wants to forgive and welcome us back.

In Exodus 34:6-7 we read:

And he passed in front of Moses, proclaiming, "The LORD, the LORD, the compassionate and gracious God, slow to anger, abounding in love and faithfulness, maintaining love to thousands, and forgiving wickedness, rebellion, and sin. Yet he does not leave the guilty unpunished; he punishes the children and their children for the sin of the parents to the third and fourth generation."

God's love is seen in that he punished to 3 or 4 generations, but his love extends to thousands. He forgives wickedness but does not let it go unpunished.

That is the point of Christmas. That is why Jesus came to earth. It was the cross at the end of his life. The cross where he died, taking the punishment that we deserved so that we could be forgiven and have our relationship with God restored.

REBUILD

We have all seen the effects of natural disasters. Whether a tsunami, an earthquake, a hurricane, a volcano or whatever else, we have all seen images and film clips of the devastation they can produce. Or possibly something very small, seemingly insignificant. Something that other people would just laugh off. You have spent ages trying to make something that has just collapsed or broken. To other people, it is trivial. But to you, it is heartbreaking. Or a relationship that has broken down. Perhaps neither of you have any real idea why, but you are not talking anymore. Or someone said or did something that really hurt you and you can't forgive.

Things break, or get broken, and need to be rebuilt.

Nehemiah was heartbroken. He was far away, in another land. A friend had just come back from home and told him that the city wall was broken down and the gates burned. His beloved hometown was in serious trouble. He sat down and wept. But he didn't stop there. He prayed and fasted. But he did not stop there. He went to the king of the land he was in and asked permission to go home and see for himself how bad things were, and to help rebuild. He was given permission and off he went. When he arrived back home, he saw things were as bad as he had been told. He spent time surveying the situation, gathered a team around him and set to work rebuilding. He faced a lot of opposition. People were actively out to attempt to destroy the work he was doing. But he persevered. He carried on praying and he carried on rebuilding. And in record time he rebuilt the entire wall and rehung the gates.

Rebuilding something can be hard work. It can be draining physically, mentally, emotionally. We cannot always do it on our own. We need help from others. We may well need help from God. So we need to come to him and ask for his help - we need to pray. But God does ask us to get involved in the rebuilding – we need to get up and follow his instructions. If Nehemiah had ignored either part his mission would have failed. If we ignore either part, then we may well fail.

God is in the business of rebuilding lives. Lives that have been knocked down through circumstances, other people's actions, or their own fault. God wants to rebuild. When Jesus was on earth he healed, he set people free from things that were holding them back, he rebuilt people's lives. It may take time. It may take a lot of effort and a lot of prayer. But that is what God wants.

And what God wants to rebuild ultimately is our relationship with him. That is why Jesus came to earth. That is why we celebrate Christmas. The Son of God left heaven with all its riches and came to live on earth and die on the cross, taking all my sin and shame on himself, taking all my brokenness, so that I could be forgiven and made whole again.

FELLOWSHIP

They had been to the big city to celebrate. They went every year. Everyone did. And they had a fantastic time, spending time with family and friends they didn't see often. And then there was the celebration. It was a special time, remembering great events of their past. They always came away feeling invigorated, with a spring in their step. They were tired, yes, but they had a new lease of life. All the time as they walked back homewards that first day there was a real buzz in their community. Everyone was so excited. They barely realised their son was not by them, but that didn't matter. He would be somewhere in their group. He would be OK.

Except, when evening came and they all stopped, he didn't turn up. They started getting concerned and asked their friends when they had last seen him. Then they became really worried. No one had seen him since they had left the big city. Everyone assumed he was with someone else, but no one had checked. In panic, the couple started running back to the big city to search for him.

For three days they searched. They looked down every alley, every dark corner where a young boy might be hiding, and they asked everyone they could if they had seen him. There was no sign of him anywhere. Finally, they made their way towards the temple, in desperation to offer up an anguished prayer for his safe return.

"Why were you searching for me?" he asked. "Didn't you know I had to be in my Father's house?"

Suddenly, it all made sense. Of course he was going to be in the temple. After all, he wasn't really her son. Yes, she had carried him for 9 months, given birth to him, fed him, looked after him and brought him up these last twelve years. But he wasn't really her son. No, he was the Son of God. And where else would the Son of God be, but in the house of God? Whose presence would he be in, if not his Father's presence? She was just there to look after him. He was a king and would be king forever. She couldn't get her head round all the things she had been told, but she could remember them all. And now, standing there, things started to make more sense. This boy was a king. He was to bring in the new kingdom of God. She felt the weight of responsibility afresh.

As she stood there she heard a voice. "Don't worry about him. I will look after him. He has a mission to accomplish and nothing can happen to him until it is finished." She felt an arm around her shoulders. She cuddled into it and felt safe, secure and loved. Then she opened her eyes and realised there was nobody there. Just her, the voice and the cuddle. Just her and God sharing a moment together.

GLORY

We all know what glory is. If is scoring a spectacular goal. It is becoming the youngest billionaire. It is reaching 1 million Instagram followers in 4 hours 1 minute. It is something spectacular.

But what is we are all wrong? What if real glory is something completely different?

In Matthew chapter 3 we read the following:

Then Jesus came from Galilee to the Jordan to be baptized by John. But John tried to deter him, saying, "I need to be baptized by you, and do you come to me?"

Jesus replied, "Let it be so now; it is proper for us to do this to fulfil all righteousness." Then John consented.

As soon as Jesus was baptized, he went up out of the water. At that moment heaven was opened, and he saw the Spirit of God descending like a dove and alighting on him. And a voice from heaven said, "This is my Son, whom I love; with him I am well pleased."

What had Jesus done that was so spectacular, so impressive that God his Father was so excited about that he had to shout from heaven so that everyone could hear? He had performed no miracle. He had healed no one. He had preached no spectacular sermon. He had done nothing.

And yet he had. He had obeyed his Father. He had obeyed God Almighty.

Jesus told a story about a rich man who went on a journey. He had 3 servants and gave them each a different amount of money. One did nothing with it, just buried in. The other 2 invested it and doubled their money. On his return, all 3 servants gave their master the original money back, plus what they had earned in the case of 2 of them. The master replied to these 2, "Well done, good and faithful servant. You have been faithful in small things; I will put you in charge of many things."

The 2 servants had been faithful. One had made 2 bags of gold profit, the other 5. But the amount didn't matter. They had used what they had wisely. They had been faithful.

Those are 2 things that will get God saying, "Well done." It is not for doing something amazing, just for obeying and being faithful. And hearing God say that should be all the glory we need, because it is the ultimate glory.

SPEAK

In Ecclesiastes 3 we read:

There is a time for everything,
  and a season for every activity under the heavens...
  a time to be silent and a time to speak.

Knowing when to be quiet and when to vocalise something can be so difficult. All too often I find myself thinking, "I should have said something there." Or, "Perhaps that was not the wisest thing to say."

Words have power. We all know that. But sometimes we underestimate how much. In the beginning, God said, "Let there be light," and there was light. Most people could probably give a time when they have been badly hurt by an unkind word, or seen their spirits soar because of something else someone has said. Words have the power to tear down and destroy, or to create something wonderful.

Jesus knew how to use words. When he spoke with the woman at the well - breaking all cultural norms because a) she was a woman and b) she was a Samaritan – he used his words to lead the conversation so that "Many of the Samaritans from that town believed in him." His words were both challenging and comforting. When he was talking with the religious leaders of the day, he could be very scathing. "You brood of vipers." "Whitewashed tombs, which look beautiful on the outside but on the inside are full of the bones of the dead and everything unclean." When confronted with a woman caught in adultery, we read "Woman, where are they? Has no one condemned you?" "No one, Sir." "Then neither do I condemn you.

Go now and leave your life of sin." He did not condemn but spoke with love and forgiveness.

How did Jesus know what to say? It's easy to say that he was God. He knew everything. Therefore of course he would know what to say. But he was also fully human, with all the weaknesses and vulnerabilities that brings. But he only spoke what he was given by his Father. He heard his Father's voice and spoke and acted on that.

He heard the voice of God. The voice that said in the beginning, "Let there be light." The voice that said, "This is my Son, whom I love; with him I am well pleased."

And that voice is still speaking. The voice that called out, "Adam, where are you?" in pain because Adam was hiding from him is still calling out to us.

In The Problem of Pain, C.S. Lewis wrote:

We can ignore even pleasure. But pain insists upon being attended to. God whispers to us in our pleasures, speaks in our conscience, but shouts in our pains: it is His megaphone to rouse a deaf world...No doubt pain as God's megaphone is a terrible instrument; it may lead to final and unrepented rebellion. But it gives the only opportunity the bad man can have for amendment. It removed the veil; it plants the flag of truth within the fortress on the rebel soul.

God's voice is there constantly. In every situation we are in. We just need to listen and learn to recognise it. We need to say, along with the young Samuel:

"Speak, for your servant is listening."

COMFORT

What would you have done?

What would you have done if you had found out the girl you were going to marry was pregnant, and you knew you weren't the father? Would you have had her stoned to death? You could have done. Would you have publicly humiliated her, telling everyone what she had done and abandoned her to whatever kind of future lay ahead for her? I could have done either. No one would have blamed me.

But, no. I decided to do something different. I loved her and wanted the best for her. No matter what had happened. I did not want to see her suffer. I couldn't marry her, but she deserved a second chance. So I decided to break off the engagement quietly and let her go, hoping that she would be able to lead some sort of normal life. I decided to tell her in the morning.

I struggled to sleep that night. I tossed and turned for hours. Had I made the right decision? Something inside me was gnawing away. As the night wore on, I became more and more uncertain. Then I fell asleep. It happened suddenly. One minute my mind was all over the place, and then I was gone. Sound asleep. Then something very unusual happened. I had a dream.

Except it was no ordinary dream. An angel from God himself appeared to me. Standing there, brilliantly white. I could barely look at him the light was so intense. "Don't worry," he said. "Take her as your wife. This child is from God, conceived of the Holy Spirit. He will give his life to save his people from their sins."

Instantly I was wide awake. But not wide awake as if woken in a mad panic. Wide awake as if I had just had the best night sleep ever. Wide awake as in completely refreshed. Wide awake without a care in the world. It made no sense. I was to take as my wife someone who was pregnant, but not with my child. What would everyone say? Would I really be able to look at her the same way again? How would I react when the child was born? There were so many questions.

Somehow, I knew that I would love her and our child more than I ever thought possible. I felt so responsible for the pair of them. This was a special child and I had to make sure that he would be safe. I had to look after and protect the two of them. My wonderful wife and our precious child. The responsibility hit me. I felt a weight growing on my shoulders, the pressure of it starting to push me down. I felt so weak, so unable to do it. It came on so suddenly, and quickly became almost unbearable. I cried out in pain. Suddenly the weight lifted.

Or perhaps, changed would be a better word. It was still there, just different. Now it was as if there was an arm around my shoulders. Supporting me. Giving me strength. I heard a quiet voice saying, "Don't worry. I am with you always." Somehow, I knew everything would be OK. Somehow, I knew this was all part of a bigger plan. Somehow, I felt at peace.

PATIENT

He had been waiting for 40 years. He knew he was destined for something special. He had known that all his life. And then he saw his chance to make a statement. He saw one of his fellow countrymen being mistreated, even more than normal. He struck out at the aggressor and killed him. He expected his fellow countrymen to rise up beside him. They were so many they had a good chance of throwing off the chains of oppression and breaking free. But it didn't work out like that. The king discovered what he had done, and no one rose up beside him. He had no choice. He had to flee. If not, he would have been the next one dead. Forty more years passed before he felt the call again. But this time it was different. He knew it was not from within. It was a call from without. The thought of going back to help his fellow countrymen gain their freedom terrified him. He tried every way he could to get out of it. But there was no way. He had to go. He had to lead his people to freedom. And after many miraculous events he did.

Before him was a couple who were promised a son. The only problem was he was about 90 and his wife 80. There was no chance. But then the option of becoming a father through his wife's servant cropped up. And he took it with both hands. The only problem was it caused so many family arguments. He regretted it deeply. If only he was waited.

1500 years later there was another man. He had to wait for 30 years. Were there any times during those 30 years when he was tempted to act? We don't know. But we do know that he didn't act until the time was right. And then he had 3 years. And everything he did was done at just the right time.

I'm also waiting. It can be hard. Sometimes it feels like nothing is happening, and the frustration kicks in as I feel like I'm going to be waiting for ever. I have to learn patience. But then things move forward, and the panic sets in. I feel like I am not ready and everything is moving too fast.

"Do you trust me when my answer is wait?"

Is lack of patience actually a lack of trust? When I get frustrated at the perceived lack of progress (or start panicking that things are moving too fast) am I really not trusting God and his timing? Because God's timing is perfect.

Galatians 4:4 says

When the right time came, God sent his son.

The right time. God always acts at the right time. God always calls at the right time. I just have to learn to trust him when things don't happen when I expect or want them.

As Gandalf the Grey said:

"A wizard is never late, Frodo Baggins. Nor is he early. He arrives precisely when he means to".

So it is with God.

MERCY

She stood there shaking in fear. She could hardly open her eyes. She could hear everyone crying out, baying for blood. Her blood. She had been caught in bed with a man who was not her husband. And that was punishable by death by stoning. She could sense everyone ready, waiting to unleash a barrage of rocks at her. She could almost smell the excitement.

But the law seemed all wrong. It was so unfair. Why was it just her? Had he not done the same thing? Was he not as guilty as she was? So why was he not about to be stoned as well? And the death penalty for just one mistake – OK, one mistake repeated several times. It seemed harsh. It seemed so unjust.

Her shaking grew worse. The waiting was unbearable. She knew there was no way out. But the stones never came. Gradually, the shouting grew less. And then, she suddenly realised there was no shouting. Everything had gone silent. She gradually opened one eye, then the other. There was no one in sight. No one, except one man. He looked at her. It was a strange look. It was a look she had never really seen before. It was a look of love and compassion.

"Where are your accusers? Didn't even one of them condemn you?"

She looked around. No one was left. "No."

"Neither do I. Go and sin no more"

She stood there, blinking. She couldn't believe it. He had shown her mercy. She knew who he was. He was a religious preacher. He should have condemned her. But he didn't. He was different. He showed her mercy, when the law condemned.

But then his words struck her. He had shown her mercy. He had not condemned, as others were. But there was a command. "Go and sin no more." His mercy had 2 consequences. She was not going to be stoned to death, like the law demanded. But she had to change. She could not carry on with the life she had been leading. His mercy compelled her to a radical about turn. She had no choice.

She stood there, blinking. But not only in shock that she was still alive. In shock at the realization of what his mercy meant. She didn't know if she had the strength to change. But she knew she had to. She knew she wanted to. And, somehow, seeing his smile and hearing his words, she knew she would.

BAPTISE

John practiced a baptism of repentance. Was it purely symbolic, an outward display of what had already happened internally, or was it more than that? Did it symbolize publicly the washing away of sins, or was it actually part of that washing process?

Philip explained the "good news about Jesus" to the Ethiopian eunuch. His immediate reaction was, "See, here is water! What prevents me from being baptized?" Was it purely symbolic, an outward display of what had already happened internally, or was it more than that? Did it symbolize publicly the washing away of sins, or was it actually part of that washing process?

Greater minds than mine have grappled with this problem and come up with differing answers. There are those who would say that it is purely a symbolic, public witness of what has already happened. And there are those who would say that it is a vital washing away of sin that is necessary for salvation. And every viewpoint in between.

For me it has to be more than just a public witness. If it were just that, why was the Ethiopian Eunuch so desperate to get baptized there and then, rather than wait until he got home? It is our response to the love of God. It is a sign of God's grace towards us. It is a washing away of sin.

But with baptism one verse came to mind:

For we were all baptized by one Spirit so as to form one body – whether Jews or Gentiles, slave or free – and we were all given the one Spirit to drink.

Whatever our belief, baptism is a sign of one thing: unity. We are baptized by one Spirit to form one body.

That speaks of unity, oneness. Obviously, if you get a group of people together you are going to have many different views. A group of football fans may all support the same team, but they may disagree about who is the best player, who should be playing that day, about a whole load of things. But ultimately that doesn't matter. They all support the same team.

I'm not saying that anything goes. Obviously there are red lines. But sometimes our red lines are not the same as God's. We need to listen carefully to differing viewpoints. We need to think about what is said and carefully weigh it up. We need to not dismiss it out of hand. We may disagree, but is it a red line? Does it create a fracture? Or is it something we can agree to disagree on, and move forward together, for "Everyone who calls on the name of the Lord will be saved." (Romans 10:13) Everyone, Jews and Gentiles. Everyone, even if they did not agree with everything Paul said.

WORD

In the beginning was the Word, and the Word was with God, and the Word was God. He was with God in the beginning. Through him all things were made; without him nothing was made that has been made. In him was life, and that life was the light of all mankind. The light shines in the darkness, and the darkness has not overcome it.

The Word became flesh and made his dwelling among us.

So starts the Gospel of John.

The Word was with God in the beginning when the universe was created. Through the Word all things were made. The Word was God himself. Almighty. All powerful. All knowing. Ever present. The mighty, majestic God. Lord over all. The creator of all things.

And yet, the Word became flesh and made his dwelling among us. This almighty, all powerful, all knowing, ever present, mighty, majestic God took on the nature of a servant, became human. He was born in humble circumstances. His family had to flee and live as refugees out of fear for their lives. He grew up and worked as a carpenter. He spent 3 years as a preacher before the tide of public opinion turned against him and he was cruelly murdered as a common criminal.

The Son of God. And yet he lived on earth as a man. The 2 don't go together. You would expect God to stay in heaven, separated from humans. Why would he want to associate with us? Why would he give up perfection to live with us, with all our problems, with all our sin?

And yet, the Word did become flesh. He did want to associate with us. Almighty God wanted to be with us. He wanted a relationship with us. He still does. That is why the Word became flesh. And he still does. That is why he came down to earth.

That is what we celebrate at Christmas. Emmanuel. God with us. Almighty God coming to earth as a baby. Throwing off all the trappings and safety of heaven to live on earth. The infinite becoming finite. The eternal becoming mortal. God becoming like me, yet somehow maintaining his perfection.

It all seems too crazy to be true. And yet, it is true. Almighty God became a vulnerable baby. I am struggling to get my head around it. Why would he do that for me?

HONEY

Psalm 119:97-104

Oh, how I love Your law!
All day long it is my meditation.
Your commandments make me wiser than my
enemies,
  for they are always with me.
  I have more insight than all my teachers,
  for Your testimonies are my meditation.
  I discern more than the elders,
  for I obey Your precepts.
  I have kept my feet from every evil path,
  that I may keep Your word.
  I have not departed from Your ordinances,
  for You Yourself have taught me.
  How sweet are Your words to my taste—
  sweeter than honey in my mouth!
  I gain understanding from Your precepts;
  therefore I hate every false way.

The bible gets a bit of a bad press. Some say it is
outdated. Others say it is full of contradictions. It is
boring, un-understandable, confusing. Completely made
up. Irrelevant.

But that is not what it says about itself. Hebrews
4:12 says:

For the word of God is alive and active. Sharper than
any double-edged sword, it penetrates even to dividing
soul and spirit, joints and marrow; it judges the
thoughts and attitudes of the heart.

It is alive and active. It penetrates deeply. On numerous occasions I – and others – have read something that has been so relevant to a particular situation, whether confronting an issue or providing an answer to a problem. It may not always feel sweet at the time when it confronts, but afterwards when the issue is sorted there is sweetness.

It provides the best moral guidance. The beatitudes (Matthew 5:1-16) provide what is widely recognised to be the best manifesto for life. Yes, parts can be confusing and difficult to understand. Yes, parts can be a bit boring. Long genealogies are not the easiest read. But everything you could want in a book is found in the bible. The story it tells is gripping. It draws you in. And no, it does not contradict itself. There are instances where that seems to be the case, but it doesn't.

What it does do is guide, provide instruction and insight, reassure and challenge. It describes the best way to live. But more than that, it talks about God, and us. It talks about a God who loves us and wants the best for us. A God who is desperate for a relationship with us. A God who wants us to know him. Not know about him but know him. It explains what the barrier is that prevents that and shows us how the barrier can be overcome. It pulls no punches but includes the promise of something much better than we could possibly imagine. It includes the promise of a kingdom where God reigns, a glorious kingdom where there is no evil and no suffering. It explains how we get there.

It is the very words of God. It is no wonder therefore that we read:

How sweet are Your words to my taste—
sweeter than honey in my mouth!

GO

When I think of GO I think of a journey. Starting where I am and ending up somewhere different. It may be going to work. It may be going to town. It may be going to see family or friends. Or on holiday somewhere. It usually involves physical movement.

But it does not have to. It can be an intellectual journey as you research something and discover new information. It can be an emotional journey as you encounter something that deeply affects you. It can also be a spiritual journey as we find beliefs challenged and altered through various circumstances.

I wonder how Mary and Joseph felt in those first few months after the angelic announcement. The news of pregnancy has quite an impact, even if you are hoping for it. What must it have been like for Mary and Joseph? Even though Joseph's initial reaction was to break the relationship and let Mary go, did it bring them closer together? How were they affected emotionally as they got used to the idea of a new member of their family? And how were their beliefs and assumptions about God challenged and altered throughout, as they came to terms with the fact that the baby that Mary was carrying was none other than the Son of God? Yes, they travelled physically. But they also journeyed in many other ways.

It is a scary thing. It is much easier just to stay where you are, not to challenge yourself intellectually, emotionally or spiritually. But if you don't, you won't grow. If you don't seek out new experiences or challenges then you will stagnate. One of the reasons for blogging Advent Word is the challenge, to be able to say something about a word someone else gives me.

Going on a journey can be exciting. It can be terrifying. It can be exhausting. It can be exhilarating. There can be boring bits. There can be times you wish it was all over and you wonder why you set out in the first place.

I set out on a journey nearly 3 years ago. I have experienced all these emotions, plus many more. For me the most terrifying step was the very first one. It was the easiest – make a simple phone call. But it terrified me. A couple of quotes helped:

A journey of 1000 miles begins with 1 simple step.
You don't have to see the whole staircase, just take the first step.

And as I took that first step I worked out where the next one was. And things became slightly easier. Each step along the way has had its share of excitement and terror. Some have been tiring. Some very difficult. Others less so. Some have made the goal seem more obvious, other less obvious. Often the thought of the destination terrifies me. But is the thing I am journeying towards really the destination? Or is it another mark of the journey?

There are so many questions. So many things I don't understand. But I set out nearly 3 years ago, and I am still journeying, still trying to find the next step. Do I regret it? Not in the slightest. It has been exhilarating.

So what am I trying to say? I guess it is, if you are feeling restless, make a change. If you feel a challenge to change something and start out on a journey, go. Think and pray about it first, to make sure it is not a really bad idea. Then start pushing at doors. Some will open, others won't. It may not be the right direction, but at least you are doing something. After all, it is easier to make a ship change direction when it is moving than when it is stationary.

REST

It has just been announced that Asda, M&S, Pets at Home and The Entertainer, along with some other shops, will remain closed on Boxing Day. I applaud that, although I question why it needs to be said. Why do shops need to state that they are going to be shut for 2 consecutive days, both of which are bank holidays? Why on earth should they be open?

What have we become as a society that we cannot cope with shops being shut for 2 days? What have we become that we need so much food that we have to buy some after 2 days? What have we become that we want to go to a clothes shop at 6am on Boxing Day for a sale? Where did we go so off course that we cannot cope without our fix of shopping?

That may sound harsh. People may well disagree with me. But for me it is a sign that we have gone absolutely crazy as a country. Yes, I often go to the Christmas sales. After a few days. Yes, I have bought things on Black Friday. Things that I have wanted. But there is no way I would take part in some of the fights I have seen on TV. I am not that desperate.

How did we become such a consumer society that we have to go out and refill our wardrobe every few months? Throwing away perfectly good clothes just because that are last season's. Why is there such a strong desire to have the latest phone, when 99% of people don't use half of the capabilities? Or any other piece of technology? Is it purely to keep up with the Jones?

I read a wonderful quote by Mahatma Gandhi the other day:

The world has enough for everyone's need, but not enough for everyone's greed.

The world can produce enough food for everyone, but people in wealthier countries overeat, leaving those in poorer countries with not enough. So we see people then spending money and time in the gym trying to get back into shape. People in wealthier countries demand produce that destroys ecosystems like rainforests, creating havoc to the poorer nations. There are enough resources in the world, but they are concentrated more and more in the hands of the few rather than being spread where they are needed.

The Isrealites had a wonderful system. Every 7 years was a sabbath year. The land was to be rested. No crops were to be grown. Then after the 7th sabbath (every 50 years) was the year of Jubilee. Everything was reset. Debts were to be cancelled. Land and property were to be given back to their original owner and things were to start again from scratch. It was to be a year of rest.

It was a system that promoted equality. It did not stop people becoming rich, but it was a constant reminder that community mattered. A strong reminder that you had to look out for the weaker in society, not let them go to the wall. It was also a strong reminder of the importance of rest and being together, not constantly rushing around.

This isn't really about Boxing Day sales and whether shops open or stay closed for 2 days, although that is a start. It is about a whole attitude. It is about taking a step back and thinking, "Do I really need that?" Or, "Do I really need to work a few extra hours today to earn more money? I have plenty, and I haven't seen my family or friends much recently, or stopped and looked after myself." It is about loving people and using things, rather than loving things and using people. It is about reassessing our priorities.

But not going shopping on Boxing Day would be a good start. Let's give shop workers a couple of day's rest. It may not work for this year, but if enough people boycott the shops this year, then next year may be different.

WORSHIP

Worship is when you are on the football terraces singing out the name of your favourite player. Worship is when you are singing along with your favourite rock band in a live concert, arms aloft. Worship is when you are in church, singing about how great God is.

But is that it? It is so easy to get caught up in the atmosphere. Sometimes we join in just so we don't feel left out. We feel on top of the world and go with the flow.

But what about those times when God feels a million miles away? What about those times when the last thing we want to do is sing about how good he is? The song is, "Forever God is faithful" and everything in you is screaming, "O no he isn't"? Can we worship in those times? What about those times when you know God is telling you to do something, and it is the last thing on earth you want to do? Go and speak with that person. Don't take that wonderful sounding job. That relationship is not right – you need to end it. What about those times? Where is worship then?

In Luke chapter 23 we read:

And He came out and went, as was His habit, to the Mount of Olives; and the disciples also followed Him. Now when He arrived at the place, He said to them, "Pray that you do not come into temptation." And He withdrew from them about a stone's throw, and He knelt down and began to pray, saying, "Father, if You are willing, remove this cup from Me; yet not My will, but Yours be done." Now an angel from heaven appeared to Him, strengthening Him. And being in agony, He was praying very fervently; and His sweat became like drops of blood, falling down upon the ground. When He rose from prayer, He came to the disciples and found them sleeping from sorrow, and He said to them, "Why are you sleeping? Get up and pray that you do not come into temptation."

Jesus was just about to be arrested and sent to the cross. He knew what was coming. Not surprisingly, he did not want to do it. He was in so much anguish that he was sweating drops of blood. But what did he say? "Yet not My will, but Yours be done." That is true worship. Following God's direction, even when everything about us is screaming to go in the opposite direction. Saying, "Forever God is faithful", even when everything about you is screaming, "No he isn't". True worship is when Horatio Spafford, after losing virtually everything he possessed, then losing his children when their ship sank was able to say, "It is well with my soul" as he passed over the place where their ship sank.
Romans chapter 12 puts it like this:

Therefore, I urge you, brothers and sisters, in view of God's mercy, to offer your bodies as a living sacrifice, holy and pleasing to God—this is your true and proper worship. Do not conform to the pattern of this world, but be transformed by the renewing of your mind. Then you will be able to test and approve what God's will is—his good, pleasing and perfect will.

That is true worship. To offer ourselves entirely to God, even in those dark, difficult situations. To be able to say along with Jesus, "Father, if You are willing, remove this cup from Me; yet not My will, but Yours be done."

PRAY

Jesus said, "When you pray....." Prayer is not an optional extra, but crucial to our Christian life. Why do so many find it so difficult? Why do I struggle so much?

I guess part of the reason is that because it is so crucial someone is out to stop us. It is done in subtle ways. Busyness. Distractions. Tiredness. I am exhausted so find it difficult to get up in the morning. And when I do get up, life can be so busy that I don't stop until I am exhausted again in the evening. If I do find 5 minutes, then my mind is often racing around on so many other things that I can't quieten it down to concentrate on God. There are classic books like "Rees Howells Intercessor." But it can appear daunting - even though I am sure it is an excellent book. I think of people like him as a great man of prayer who would put me to shame, but fail to think that he must have started somewhere. At one point he must have made his first faltering steps in prayer. He must have felt he made many mistakes. He must have felt that he was talking to a void or a brick wall many times.

Champions are not born. Yes, some people have more natural ability than others, but champions are not the people who never fail, but the people who never quit.

That is the secret. Keep trying. If something doesn't work, try something else. Not necessarily immediately. Give it a good go. But ultimately, if something isn't working then move on. A liturgy can be very helpful. In those times when things are dry and difficult, I find praying those words that millions of people have prayed over hundreds of years helps. Keep persevering, even when times are tough. Even 2 minutes is better than nothing. Prayer is about talking with God. It is a conversation. It is about spending time with him. It is something he wants, something he delights in. It is not something that you have to force on God. He wants to hear us. He wants to speak to us. As in any relationship, he delights in our presence. The feeling I get when I spend time with my wife is nothing on how God feels when we spend time with him.

Yes. I find prayer difficult. Yes, it can seem dry, as if I am shouting at nothing. But then there are those times when I can feel the presence of God so clearly. Or I hear him speaking to me. Those times make the difficult ones worthwhile.

It is still difficult though. Getting up in the mornings is never easy. My bed is always so much more appealing. But on those occasions when I join Jesus in getting up early and going to a quiet place to pray can be so special.

LEARN

Learning is difficult. Learning facts is one thing. Some people can do it easily, others find it much more difficult. Then there is learning what the facts actually mean. That can be so much more difficult. It is so easy to see the facts and come up to a completely different meaning to someone else. I think we are seeing this at the moment with the Presidential election in the USA. On one side you have Democrats. The vote was perfectly legal and proper. Their man won. They are happy. On the other side are the Republicans. Their man didn't lose. The election was stolen from him. There was widespread fraud. Both sides are seeing the same information, but they are believing different things. It feels like both sides are believing what they want to believe. There are dissenters, those Republicans who accept that the Democrats won. It is difficult to tell how widespread they are. The news coverage of Republicans shows them mainly crying out "Stop the steal." But are we seeing the majority of Republicans, or just the fanatical few? I have learnt to take news coverage with a pinch of salt sometimes.

I think a lot of what we "learn", especially as adults, can come about because we read what we already believe into the facts that we see. How often are we truly startled by something and change our opinion? How often do we say, "I was wrong. There is another way. There is another viewpoint that is equally valid."?

I have been doing that a lot recently. Unlearning a lot of things I had learnt when I was younger. Things I had been told that were actually wrong. It has been a challenge, and continues to be a challenge. If I had come at things with the mindset, "I am right and other ideas are wrong," then I would have got nowhere.

17th December

Probably I would not have changed at all. I have had to come at things with an open mind, saying, "What is this alternative opinion? Can I make sense of it?"

That is the secret. Having an open mind. Wondering. Asking the questions and genuinely wanting to find out the answers. Being prepared to change, rather than being closed-minded and refusing to believe that you may be wrong or may not know everything. It can be a scary place to find yourself. But equally the rewards can be great. There is a balance to strike so that your mind isn't so open and porous that anything can get in, or fall out. There do need to be some balances and checks, or some non-negotiables.

It is always good to look at familiar things again. The Christmas story is familiar. But how much of it do we understand? How much do we gloss over? How much do we really appreciate what happened? Two things have struck me this Advent. The first, on reading John chapter 1 and Hebrews chapter 1, was how much the Christmas story is rooted in Israel's history, and right back to the beginning of time. Creation itself. Jesus' birth, life, death and resurrection were not afterthoughts. They were not a Plan B when everything went wrong. They were all part of God's plan from the very start. The second thing is fear. We are living in strange times. People are, quite rightly, fearful of the future. How did Mary and Joseph feel? Did Mary fear that Joseph would abandon her? Did they both feel what others would say about Mary's pregnancy? Did they fear the journey to Bethlehem? Did they fear the birth? Did they fear for their lives as they fled to Egypt? Were they ever free from that fear? And yet, they kept going. Despite that fear they knew God's presence and guidance. They knew his protection. And so can we.

We always have things to learn, as long as we have open minds and take a fresh look.

BLESS

Jesus makes it clear that he wants to bless. The sermon on the mount in Matthew chapter 5 starts with a whole load of statements, each of which starting with, "Blessed are..." But some of them sound a bit strange. Blessed are the poor in spirit – those who realise they have nothing, that they need God at every stage of their lives, that they need his forgiveness. This goes against modern ideas of self-reliance. Blessed are those who mourn – those who are grieved by the state of the world or their own lives, those who realise that major change is necessary, those who don't follow the crowd. Rather than go with the flow and blend in for an easy life they want to make a radical change. Blessed are those who hunger and thirst for righteousness – those whose motivation is for things to be right, to be free from sin or guilt. Not pleasure seeking, not taking the easy way out but striving to live a life free from sin, even if it means being left out by others. Blessed are you when people persecute you because of Jesus. The list goes on.

These all seem backwards. The world tells us that we should strive after a better job, more money. But Jesus said, "But seek first his kingdom and his righteousness, and all these things will be given to you as well."

Jesus' teaching seems upside down. It goes against what the world says so often. But then, so did Jesus. He came from heaven. He was God. He emptied himself of all his outward glory by reducing himself to the form of a lowly servant. He became human. More than that, he became a weak, vulnerable baby. Someone completely reliant on others to look after him. Not what we would expect. And his life and teaching were equally radical. He initiated a conversation with a Samaritan woman, which was unheard of for a Jewish man at the time. He spent time with the outcast, the lowest in society, those the religious leaders would have nothing to do with. One of Jesus' teachings is, "Whoever wants to be my disciple must deny themselves and take up their cross and follow me." Not what the world preaches.

But the thing is, when we do these things, we are blessed. When we do these things, God looks on us and says, "Well done." God looks on us and smiles. We have divine favour. Because that is what blessing is. It is not a massive bank balance. It is not an easy life. The apostles proved that. They suffered massive persecution and most, if not, all were martyred. Blessing does not mean an easy life. But it does mean receiving the favour of God. It does mean experiencing his presence. It does mean knowing him.

But it does also sometimes mean that things mysteriously work in our favour. An unexpected treat arrives. I can remember receiving £5 in the post 31 years ago, and feeling really blessed by it. It was just what I needed, a reminder that God had not forgotten me. Something happens that never should, but is exactly what you need at that time. I can remember just making a boat trip in Kenya that we should have missed, and getting up close to some hippos. It was an amazing experience. Some people may say things like these are coincidences, but it felt that God was certainly smiling on us on that occasion.

Blessing will come when we forget everything and follow Jesus, wherever he leads us.

TURN

We've been on several walks this year. More so than normal because we've had more time due to lock down. It has been lovely exploring the surrounding area. Most of the time we've known where we were and the way to go, but once or twice we've realised we have been off course. We took a wrong turning and needed to turn back to get on the right path.

In life, we try to keep on the "straight and narrow." We endeavour to do what is right. But sometimes/often I know I mess things up and get it wrong. Sometimes it is a case of "Oops. I should not have done that. I won't do it again." But other times it is more fundamental. It is a habit that I have or something that I automatically do that I know needs changing. And that can be really difficult. Jesus put it this way in Matthew 5v30:

And if your right hand causes you to stumble, cut it off and throw it away. It is better for you to lose one part of your body than for your whole body to go into hell.

That seems drastic, and I don't see many people wandering around with only one hand. So either we are all perfect (which I do not believe to be the case, for me anyway), we don't take the bible seriously (I will reserve judgement on that one, but not only for this reason), or this is not meant to be taken literally. So what does it mean?

I think this is wonderfully illustrated by a story I read years ago. I think I read it in Adrian Plass' Second Sacred Diary. I recommend his books to anyone. They are funny, light-hearted but then you realise he has slipped in a serious point. One that you will remember years later. It goes something like this:

There was a couple who had been married for a few years. Then she got a new job that involved commuting via train. Each day she got up and caught the same train. And after a while, she recognised the same people on the train. Especially one man. He was always on the train before her, but she always got on and sat at the same table as him. It started off as a nod. Then a smile. Then a few words. Nothing serious. There was never any intention to take things further. They just chatted a bit. Then, one day, he was not on the train. Her heart sank a bit. He wasn't there for a few days, and she started feeling a bit depressed. But the next Monday when she got on the train, there he was again. Her heart skipped in delight at seeing him again. But then she broke out in a cold sweat. What was going on? Was she falling in love with him? But she loved her husband and had no intention of leaving him, or starting an affair. What should she do?

She spent the rest of the day in turmoil. When she got home, she knew what she had to do. After dinner, when she and her husband were sitting down sharing a drink, she told him exactly what was going on, and her fears. She looked at him, slightly fearful, not knowing what his reaction would be. He sat there and puffed slowly on his pipe for a minute. (For some reason I can distinctly remember that he smoked a pipe.) Then he said 2 words. "Change trains."

It was that simple. She was in a predicament. If she carried on as she had been, who knows what may have happened. But the solution was simple. Change trains. Get out of that situation.

I think that I what Jesus meant by, "And if your right hand causes you to stumble, cut it off and throw it away." I don't think he meant that we should start cutting off various limbs. But I do think he meant if a situation is causing you problems, if the temptation to sin is great, then get out of that situation. If going into a certain shop means that you are too tempted to steal something, don't go into that shop. Not alone, at least. If hanging around that group of friends means that you find it really difficult not to join in with things you know to be wrong, change friends. If catching that train means you are becoming too close to that person, then change trains.

REJOICE

One thing I don't like about this time of year is the majority of Christmas songs. We are constantly bombarded by songs telling us that this is the most wonderful time of year. The happiest time of year. Everything is so jolly. We are not allowed to feel down. We are not allowed to worry. We can all stick on a silly hat and blow an out-of-tune plastic whistle and everything will be OK.

Another thing is the incessant adverts. Fortunately I have not seen many this year, primarily because we are watching very little live TV and not really going out, but I know they are out there. They always are. This is the must-have present. Buy this and everything will be OK. The problem is, the must-have present is unobtainable because everyone else wants it. So panic kicks in. What you buy does not make everything OK.

No, I'm not becoming a misery. I do enjoy the trimmings that come with Christmas. But there is another side. The people who are severely depressed, who stick on a plastic smile and pretend that everything is OK, but who are screaming in agony inside. The people who have painful memories of loved ones who are no longer with them. People who have nothing, yet feel forced into buying what they cannot afford by adverts, pressure from children or others, suffering the financial consequences for months to come. People who cannot afford to buy presents for their children, so wrap up empty boxes so at least they have something to open on Christmas day. And yes, they do exist. People who buy a little to eat, but then cannot afford to heat their home. Charities have provided an unprecedented number of food hampers this year, and are providing the same over Christmas. And now we are going into a period of tighter lockdown, just as Christmas is approaching. We can spend much less time, or even no time, with family and friends we don't live with or who are not in our bubble.

Looking at the world it can be so difficult to rejoice. And yet, Christmas is a time for rejoicing, for celebration.

It is a time we can celebrate the birth of a baby. A baby who was born to be saviour of the world. A baby who was born with one main purpose – to die. To take our guilt and our sin and to give us forgiveness. To enable us to be in a right relationship with God, the creator of the universe. To enable us to become whole again, to remove all the tensions and strains that I can feel because I look at my life and know that it is not what it should be. To set me free from things that hold me back. From hurts, whether caused by others, circumstances or self-inflicted. To give me real, deep, everlasting joy, not plastic, fleeting happiness. No matter what the circumstances. To bring me a new life.

But things do not end there. It is not just about me. It is not just about making me feel good and bringing me joy. It compels me to bring that joy to others. It compels me to work to bring freedom to others. To help release them from things that bind them, whether poverty or hurts. Whether hopelessness or frustration with life. As God works in me, changing me, I am compelled to fight to see change in the world. I may not feel there is much I can do. It may be in only a small way. But many small changes create a big difference. Many small victories can bring about the correction of massive injustices. And that is worth rejoicing over.

MYSTERY

Sitting here, looking at a model nativity on the desk I am struck by a question. Why? Why did God send his son to earth? Why did he come? Why?

It seems crazy. Right in the beginning there was only 1 rule. Do not eat the fruit from this tree. Adam and Eve could do anything else, but they were not allowed to eat from that one tree. And what did they do? They ate the fruit from that one tree. They broke the one rule. Then the blame game started, as Adam blamed Eve and Eve blamed the snake. Adam blamed God. It was not a good start.

Things didn't get any better. Soon there was jealousy and murder. Soon, every inclination of the thoughts of the human heart was only evil all the time. After a reset, things didn't get much better. People's behaviour went from bad to worse. Even when God called out a people of his own, he found them to be stubborn and stiff-necked. They constantly rebelled. They were never faithful for long, but constantly chased after other experiences, other leaders, other gods. God's heart was broken time and time again. No matter what he did his people did not remain faithful to him for long. He blessed them, and they strayed. He sent them into exile, and they turned their backs on him.

So why did Jesus come? Why did God take such a dangerous course to win his people back? So much could have gone wrong. There was no guarantee that Mary would accept so readily God's plan. Joseph could easily have had Mary stoned for adultery. Herod could have succeeded in killing Jesus before he had a chance in life. And Jesus was human. He was tempted, just as we are. At any point he could have got it wrong, he could have sinned. Then he would not have been the perfect sacrifice. He could have given in to Satan's temptations in the desert just after he was baptized. He could have given up right at the end of his life when he prayed "Let this cup be taken from me." But he didn't. He then prayed, "Yet not my will be done, but yours." So much could have gone wrong. If anything had, then Satan would have won. God would have been defeated.

But nothing went wrong. Everyone got it right. Jesus triumphed.

But why did God do it? Why did God take such a risky plan? Why did he even want to, seeing how humankind treated, and still does treat, him? Why would a perfect, holy God want anything to do with mankind, let alone go to such extreme lengths to have a relationship with us?

To me, that is the mystery above all mysteries. I often look at myself and this world and wonder, Why? Why would he want to do that? The only answer I have can be summed up in 3 simple words. God is love. Not God loves. But God is love. He can do nothing but love. And His love drove Him to extreme lengths to enable me to have a relationship with him. Even becoming like me, being born in Bethlehem, living on earth and dying. What other religion has a God who does that? What other religion has a God who loves to that extent, that he is prepared to die to save mankind?

WISDOM

Knowledge says that a tomato is a fruit. Wisdom knows that they go better with lettuce than strawberries.

I love that simple definition of knowledge and wisdom. I have heard it completed by the phrase, And philosophy asks whether ketchup is a smoothie. For me it explains it so well. Knowledge knows the facts. Wisdom knows how to use or apply them.

You can know everything there is to know about something, but not understand it. Or your knowledge can be a bit patchy, but you get what you know. Who is likely to do better?

There was a top physicist called Richard Feynman. At one time he taught somewhere in South America I think it was. The students there got fantastic grades in their exams. But then they started jobs and really struggled to do anything. They had been taught the facts. They had been taught how to answer the exam questions. But they did not understand what they knew. They had no wisdom. He told another story about one university department that had a brand new, flashy piece of equipment. Another department had a very old version. It was a mess with wires all over the place. It looked like it was just about to break down all the time. But which one got the better experimental results? The old, clapped out one. Why? Because it was built with love, care and attention. And its operators understood it and how to use it. They had wisdom.

In the book of James, chapter 2 verse 19 we read:

You believe that there is one God. Good! Even the demons believe that--and shudder.

Yes, even the demons know the facts. They have the knowledge. But they don't get it. They do not have the wisdom that it takes. We may know everything there is to know about Christianity. Our theology may be perfect. We may know everything there is to know about God. But it makes no difference. Knowledge gets us nowhere. No, I am not saying that knowledge is useless. But knowledge will get us nowhere with God. For that we need wisdom. For that we need our eyes to be opened. And there is only one way for that to happen. Colossians 1:9-14 says:

For this reason, since the day we heard about you, we have not stopped praying for you. We continually ask God to fill you with the knowledge of his will through all the wisdom and understanding that the Spirit gives, so that you may live a life worthy of the Lord and please him in every way: bearing fruit in every good work, growing in the knowledge of God, being strengthened with all power according to his glorious might so that you may have great endurance and patience, and giving joyful thanks to the Father, who has qualified you to share in the inheritance of his holy people in the kingdom of light. For he has rescued us from the dominion of darkness and brought us into the kingdom of the Son he loves, in whom we have redemption, the forgiveness of sins.

We need to come to God and ask for his wisdom, for he is the only one who can reveal things to us. And when we do that and keep doing that, we can be sure that he will answer and give us all good things.

HOLY

Holiness is, to a large extent, laughed at today. Holiness is thought of as slightly strange. It brings up images of someone in a long, white linen gown. They are probably wearing sandals that were possibly in fashion in 1970, and white socks. They might have a long, straggly beard. They go about with a slightly wimpy grin on their face and utter, "Bless you my child" at everyone they pass. They are probably wimpy in character as well. They are probably condescending, self-absorbed and judgmental. A killjoy. The list could go on.

But is that what holiness is all about? Is that really what God wants of us?

I think holiness comes about when we are set apart for God, when we let him take control of our lives, when we become more like him, when our union with him is increasing. And surely the best example is Jesus, fully God and also fully human.

Jesus, the one who changed water into the best wine. Jesus, the one who healed many and who raised Lazarus from the dead. Jesus, who made a whip and chased merchants from the temple, overturning their tables as he went. Jesus, who called the religious leaders of the day "whitewashed tombs", looking great on the outside but full of dead man's bones. Jesus, whose teaching was controversial, who stirred up trouble wherever he went. Jesus, who lost many followers because his teaching was too harsh for them. Jesus, who didn't condemn but forgave the woman caught in adultery. Jesus, who is so far removed from the stereotypical image of holiness. Jesus, who is constantly calling us to follow him.

But why don't we? Why don't we grasp this image and make it our heart's desire? Jesus' life was the most eventful, most fulfilled life every lived. Why don't we desire that for ourselves?

It could be fear. We are afraid of what it will mean. What will God ask of me? What will he want to change? Where will he ask me to go? It is pretty much guaranteed to be scary and difficult. But he promises to be with us all the time, wherever we go. He promises to guide us. He promises to be our strength. He promises to give us the words we need at the right time.

It could be that we don't feel we are worth it. We are such terrible people that there is no way we could ever be holy. We are so sinful that God would want nothing to do with us. Yes, it is true that our sin creates a barrier between us and God. But that was why Jesus came. His death took away the curse that we deserved. He took the punishment so we didn't have to, so we could be forgiven. There was no way we could earn our way to God, so he came to us.

Being holy is not being perfect. Yes, we will mess things up. Yes, we will sin. That much is guaranteed. But another thing that is guaranteed is that when we repent, God will forgive us. Being holy is setting our lives apart for God. Being holy is letting God rule in our lives more and more. Being holy is becoming more like Jesus. Being holy is becoming more the person we are supposed to be.

PROCLAIM

On that night the shepherds were in the fields. Suddenly an angel appeared in the sky and they were terrified. The angel told them not to be afraid. They were to go to Bethlehem to see the baby who had been born, the Messiah. The Saviour. Suddenly a great company of angels appeared and praised God:

Glory to God in the highest heaven,
  and one earth peace to those on whom his favour rests.

The shepherds rushed to Bethlehem and found the baby. They were amazed and told everyone what they had seen.

Proclaim. To announce officially or publicly. To indicate clearly.

The carol goes, "How silently, how silently, the wonderous gift is given." But that is not how God works. He works by announcing his plans through his prophets. He won't do anything unless it is announced. That is not his way. He is about relationships. He is about taking with his people. He wants to let us know his plans. More so than we are ready to hear them. This was often the case with the Old Testament prophets. They warned the Israelites, but were usually ignored. But God kept on. More prophets came. But they were ignored as well, or killed. And God's heart was broken. He was desperate for his people to hear his voice and to respond. But they didn't. But that didn't stop him trying.

God hasn't changed. He is still talking today. He still uses his people to proclaim his message. But sometimes we don't pass it on. Sometimes we don't realise what he is asking us to say or do. We don't listen well enough.

We don't expect him to speak to us. We don't recognise his voice when he does. There is so much noise in our minds that we can't decipher his quiet voice.

But God still proclaims. He always will.

I miss so much of what he is saying. My mind is so full of stuff that I can't work out which is his voice. Somehow I need to learn to quieten down my mind. I need to find that place of peace and quiet, so that I can hear his still, small voice. But I need to do more than that. It is one thing to hear the voice of God. What good would it have done if the shepherds had said, "Thanks for the message. That is great news. Now can we carry on watching our sheep?"? No, they had to respond. It is the same with me. I have to respond to God's voice. It is not always easy, but I need to do it. For that is why God speaks.

God proclaims so that we know what he is going to do, so that we are ready for him.

And the last proclamation of Jesus in the bible? It is his Second Coming, when he will come to judge the living and the dead. Will we be ready for him?

"Yes, I am coming soon."

IMMANUEL – GOD WITH US

Christmas 2020 is going to be different. It is not what anyone expected, or wanted. But then, the birth of Jesus was not what was expected either.

Mary was a good girl. There was no way she would have had a child out of wedlock. But she was pregnant. Joseph had to face the fact that his fiancée was pregnant, and he wasn't the father. Neither of them had planned this.

Sometimes life throws stuff at us. Whether it is COVID or something else, things happen that have the potential to knock us completely off course.

But what did Mary and Joseph discover? They heard the voice of God saying, "Don't worry". They both discovered the God of comfort. They both felt his reassuring presence with them. It wasn't easy for them. There would have been talking behind their backs, or to their faces. There would have been name calling, insults, people looking the other way. But they knew God was with them.

That is one thing that has struck me this Advent. My God is an almighty God. He is the creator of the universe. He is above all things. And yet, he is the God of comfort. He is the God who will come along one solitary human who is having a tough time, put his arm around them and give them a hug. He is the God who will strengthen us when we feel weak. He is the God who will speak. Words of comfort. Words of love. Words of compassion. Words of strength. He is the God who, when we feel we have really blown it, forgives us when we repent. He is the God whose heart breaks when we ignore him but rejoices when we turn back to him. He is the God who longs for a relationship with us. He longs to communicate with us, to share his plan for us.

But the point of Christmas is Easter. The problem of man's sin needed to be dealt with for us to be able to have that relationship with God. A holy God can't be with a sinful people. Sin had to be dealt with. Someone had to die. And that person was Jesus, both fully human and fully God. He took the punishment I deserved. This is how I can now be forgiven. This is how I can now have my relationship with God restored.

Yes, Christmas is about a baby in a manger. But it is about so much more than that. It is about how much God loves us and cares for us. It is about this God of love making a way so that we can have a restored relationship with him, if we so choose. It is about God coming to dwell with us. So this Christmas let us remember one thing. Things are different. Things are difficult. But the baby in the manger shows us one thing:

Immanuel – God with us.

THE PILGRIMAGE CONTINUES

I recently did something I have been wanting to do for many years. I walked the Pilgrim Way to Lindisfarne. It was part of a day walk from Fenwick, which in turn was part of a longer pilgrimage walk from Gainsford, near Darlington. I would have loved to walk more, but life got in the way. The weather was pretty good for the second half of September and it was a very enjoyable day, walking and talking with a wide mix of people, most of whom I had never met before. And will probably never meet again.

But that is how life goes. We spend years with some people, while others we know for a very short time. And sometimes it is these people who make a lasting impression. Sometimes it is just one comment that you overhear in someone else's conversation that hits you. That is what happened that day. It was a line I overheard, and I have no idea what the context was. But it set off a train of thought in my mind that later that day before leaving the island I had to write down:

The Pilgrim's Way

I can't remember her exact words, but it was something like, "It's hard to remember to lift your eyes up to see the wonderful view." I was crossing the Pilgrim's Way to Lindisfarne, having joined the last day of the Lindisfarne Gospel Pilgrimage. There were about 30 of us making the crossing, all barefoot. From a distance it looks easy, walking across some sand following some large wooden posts to make sure you don't go off course. But as I started I realised it wasn't that easy. Some of the sand was fairly solid and OK for walking on. For a few steps. Until I came to some sand that was slightly wetter. When I hit that sand my feet started slipping around and there were a couple of occasions when I nearly ended up flat on my back. Some areas had plant growth. Sea Asparagus I think I heard someone say. That wasn't too bad, but there could be some sharp bits that pricked my feet. And then back onto the sand which was damp, and therefore slippery, covered in sharp shells and also comprising of a thin layer of sand with black sludge under. Black sludge which made anything slippery.

When I heard that comment I was walking through one of the many streams that wind their way across the Pilgrim's Way. That was actually the easiest part of the walk. The one time when I could look up to admire the view in confidence.

"Then he brought me back to the entrance of the temple; there, water was flowing from below the threshold of the temple towards the east (for the temple faced east); and the water was flowing down from below the south end of the threshold of the temple, south of the altar."

This is the start of Ezekiel chapter 47. Ezekiel is describing a vision he had of a river flowing from the very throne of God, getting deeper and deeper until it was deep enough to swim in. It was a river that provided food and nourishment to the banks, where there was great growth, as well as being full of fish and life itself.

That comment I overheard suddenly made sense. While I was been walking on the sand or vegetation, I had to be very careful where I put my feet. I had to keep my eyes focused on the ground to make sure I didn't slip or cut my foot open on a sharp shell. But when I was walking in the stream things were completely different. I had confidence. My feet suddenly felt a lot warmer. I felt secure. In some ways it felt that a burden was lifted from me, almost like the stream was giving me life.

Life from the stream. Life from the river flowing from God's throne. Thoughts of that river have been floating around the back of my mind for the last few days. I can't remember how they got there. But I suddenly realised why. And I was receiving a personal demonstration. Walking in the river that flows from God's throne is the best place to walk. Gaining life and energy from God's Spirit keeps us going. It is the safest place to be.

I am sitting here, looking towards Lindisfarne and Bamburgh Castles, further out to the Farne Isles and beyond to the expanse of the North Sea. It is so peaceful. The only sounds I can hear are birds, the wind, and the sea gently lapping at the shore. I am really enjoying a few minutes peace before having to go back to the real world. And I am wondering how much longer would that peace last if I soaked myself in the river of God. And how much more I would enjoy the view if I could lift my eyes away from my feet because I knew I was walking in a safe, secure place.

People talk about special places, places where they can feel God. For me, Lindisfarne is one of those. I feel cut off from the stresses and strains of live and in the presence of something, or someone, special. I feel free. Whether it is because when I am on the island I can be cut off from the mainland, cut off from reality; or the fact that there has been fervent prayer on the island for centuries; or another reason, I don't know. But it has been a special place for me since I first visited. And on that day, as I walked a walk I had been wanting to walk for years, one half-heard comment made all the difference.

And so, the pilgrimage continues. Where it will lead, I don't know. But one thing I do know. I need to keep walking in those streams flowing from the throne of God.

AFTERTHOUGHT

I said at the start that I had found re-reading these both encouraging and challenging. I feel that I have heard the voice of God again. I have heard his still, small voice calling me into a deeper relationship with him. He loves me. He delights in me. He wants an intimate relationship with me. And that just blows my mind. Almighty God. Creator God. All-powerful God. All-knowing God. I could go on. This is the one who wants an intimate relationship with me. And as I carry on along my pilgrimage, I am discovering more and more that I need that intimate relationship. For wisdom. For guidance. For strength. I know if I keep going along this road by myself, I will fall flat on my face. I will break. I know the only way forward is with Him. In close contact with Him at all times. I am finding more and more that I want to feel an arm around my shoulders, to feel safe, secure and loved. I want to share a moment with God. I want, and need, to feel his support, to hear his quiet voice saying, "Don't worry. I am with you always." And the only way I will know that is by being with Him.

Even youths grow tired and weary,
    and young men stumble and fall;
but those who hope in the Lord will renew their strength.
    They will soar on wings like eagles;
    they will run and not grow weary,
    they will walk and not be faint.

**I lift my eyes to the mountains –
Where does my help come from?
My help comes from the Lord,
The Maker of heaven and earth
Psalm 121:1-2**

Musings of a Pilgrim continues to be published as a personal blog on Facebook and can be contacted by email on musingsofapilgrim15@gmail.com

https://www.facebook.com/profile.php?id=1000272137 16719

Printed in Great Britain
by Amazon

87756905R00047